The Theory of Permanent Revolution by Nikolai Bukharin
First Prism Key Press Edition 2011

Prism Key Press
New York, NY 10001
PrismKeyPress.com

ISBN-13: 978-1467902717

The Theory of
Permanent Revolution

Nikolai Bukharin

CONTENTS

Introduction by the Editor of the *Communist Review*

Nikolai Ivanovich Bukharin, the author of the following article, was born in 1888. His father being a college professor, young Bukharin passed through the municipal school, and from there to the college where he finished his secondary studies. He next went to the Faculty for Law in the University of Moscow, and worked one year in the Faculty for Law in the University of Vienna.

Bukharin joined the Social-Democratic Party (Bolshevik) in 1906, at the age of 18 years, and from that time devoted all his energy to the service of the Party and of revolutionary action.

After 1905, the revolutionary movement passed through a period of depression and stagnation, particularly following the massacre at Lena. The intellectuals were then frightened by the Czarist Terror, the advanced workers watched and pursued by the police. During these years it was particularly difficult for the revolutionaries to work. Nevertheless, Bukharin continued to be very active.

He helped to organize numerous economic and political strikes of the factory workers in Moscow and St Petersburg (now Leningrad), took part in all the student movements, in the celebrations of the first of May, mass meetings and other activities. In 1908, he was elected to the Moscow Committee of the Party. In 1910 he was arrested by the Moscow police for his revolutionary activity and after a year's imprisonment he was deported to Siberia.

Escaping from Siberia, he went abroad and remained abroad till 1917. He lived in a number of countries, in Germany, Austria, Switzerland, Sweden, Norway and America. It was while he was abroad that he made the acquaintance of Lenin, with whom he remained a devoted disciple. He occupied himself with the agitation and propaganda of Bolshevism, and took an active part in the international working-class movement. In the course of his peregrinations in the different countries, he carried on revolutionary propaganda amongst the workers in Germany, Austria, America, etc, organising a large number of workers' study circles. At the same time, he employed himself in literature and displayed the qualities of a talented writer and Marxist theoretician. An eminent Bolshevik, Bukharin took part in many of the conferences of the Party.

In the early part of 1917, he returned to Russia. At Moscow, he became editor of the *Social-Democrat* and the reviews *Spartacus* and *The Communist*. While he devoted the most of his time to literary activity, he never neglected the practical work among the proletariat of Moscow. Under the Provisional Government, he conducted a fierce controversy against the conciliations. In 1918, he became Editor of the *Pravda*.

After the October Revolution his literary activity increased. In 1918, he was made a member of the collegium for editing the State edition [sic — MIA], and continued as a member till 1921. In the year 1918, he began his pedagogical career. He was in charge of the First State University of Moscow, and of the Sverdlov University. He was also a member of the Presidium of the Socialist Academy. At the same time he continued his functions as Editor of *Pravda*.

At the Sixth Congress of the Party in 1917, Bukharin was elected to the Central Committee of the Russian Communist Party. Since 1918 he has been a member of the Pan-Russian Central Executive Committee, since 1917 a member of the Moscow Soviet, and since 1919 a member of the Presidium of the Communist International.

His chief writings are:

* *The ABC of Communism* (in collaboration with

Preobrazhensky)

* *The Crisis of Capitalism and the Communist Movement* (1923)
* *World Economy and Imperialism*
* *The Revolution and Proletarian Culture* (1923)
* *The Theory of Historical Materialism*
* *The Programme of Communism*
* *From the Overthrowal of Czarism to the Collapse of the Bourgeoisie*
* *The Economics of the Transition Period* (1920)
* *The Political Economy of the Rentier*

In addition, Comrade Bukharin has written a number of other works on economic and political questions.

In the recent Trotsky discussion, Bukharin made a report on 13 December 1924, to a meeting of the propagandists of the Moscow organization on 'The Theory of Permanent Revolution'. The following article is taken from that report and is a brilliant contribution to the theory and practice of Leninism.

8

The General Estimation of Our Revolution

We come now to the general estimation of our revolution. Comrade Trotsky's theory is called the 'Theory of Permanent Revolution'. We have before us, above all, the question of the general estimation of our revolution. Comrade Trotsky, in one of his last, or 'last but one', productions, in his pamphlet *The New Course*, in this connection wrote the following:

As for the theory of permanent revolution, *I see absolutely no reason for repudiating what I wrote about it in 1904-05-06, and later.* Even now, I con- sider that *the fundamental direction of the ideas that it developed at that time is incomparably nearer to the real essence of Leninism* than very much of what was written by a number of Bolsheviks at that time. The term *permanent revolution* [NB — Italics are ours] is Marx's term. Translated precisely, permanent revolution means constant and unceasing revolution. What political idea is contained in these words? The idea that for us, for Communists, the revolution does not come to an end after one or other political gain has been achieved, but develops further, and for us the limits for it are the establishment of Socialist society... In the conditions prevailing in Russia this implied, not a bourgeois republic as a political achievement, and not even the democratic dictatorship of the proletariat and peasantry, but a Workers' Government relying upon the support of the peasantry and the starting point of an era of international Socialist revolution... *Consequently, the idea of permanent revolution completely and wholly coincides with the fundamental strategical policy of Bolshevism... No attempt at minimizing the importance of the peasantry was made in any of my writings at that time. The path of 'permanent revolution' led straight to Leninism, and particularly to the theses of April 1917.* (*The New Course*, published by Krassnaya, November 1924, page 50) [1]

10

In the preface to his book *1905*, Comrade Trotsky wrote:

The views of the character of the revolutionary development of Russia, which had received the appellation of the theory of 'permanent revolution', developed in the mind of the writer in the interval between 9 January and the April strikes of 1905. Although with some interruptions *this estimation has been confirmed completely throughout the course of 12 years.* (*1905*, second edition, Gosizdat, 1922, preface, pp 4-5) [2]

Finally, in his letter to Comrade Olminsky, Comrade Trotsky says:

I do not consider that in my disagreements with the Bolsheviks I was altogether wrong... I consider that *my estimation of the motive forces of the revolution was absolutely correct...*

Even now I could without difficulty divide my polemic articles against the Mensheviks and the Bolsheviks into two categories. (1) *Those devoted to an analysis of the inherent forces of the revolution and its perspectives...* and (2) devoted to the estimation of the factions among the Russian Social-Democrats, their antagonisms, etc. The articles of the first category I could submit even now without alteration, *for they wholly and completely coincide with the position of our party taken up since 1917.* [3]

Thus, Comrade Trotsky now asserts that:

1. The theory of permanent revolution has proved to be correct, for it has been confirmed by experience 'wholly and completely'.
2. The theory of permanent revolution is infinitely nearer to the essentials of Leninism than all the rest.
3. The theory of permanent revolution is in complete harmony with the strategical policy of our party and that of Bolshevism taken up since 1917.
4. The theory of permanent revolution under no circumstances is based upon an underestimation of the

peasantry, and generally that:

5. The theory of permanent revolution presents an absolutely correct estimation of the motive forces of our revolution.

In paying so many compliments to his theoretical offspring, Comrade Trotsky to a high degree reveals his *internal party policy*.

Why is the whole history of our Party right up to 1917, in the eyes of Comrade Trotsky, equal to zero? Because, in his opinion, in 1917 the Party adopted the point of view of permanent revolution. Why indeed was our Party 'born' in 1917? Because only at that time was it re-baptised with the sign of the permanent revolution. Why is it unimportant to deal with the pre-revolutionary fight against Menshevism and Trotskyism? Because the theory of permanent revolution acts as a screen to conceal the past, present and future errors of Comrade Trotsky. And so on, and so forth.

To sum up: the essence of Leninism, of that born *as Leninism* in 1917 (see also 'Nearer in Spirit' article of Comrade Preobrazhensky) *is the theory of Permanent revolution*. It is not surprising, therefore, that Comrade Trotsky comes forth as the chief Leninist and guardian of its covenants (out of modesty he does not claim to be their authority). What is important for Comrade Trotsky is not historical Bolshevism, but Trotskyism labelled Leninism.

But we will leave this question now, for it has been sufficiently dealt with already in our press. We will take up the analysis of Comrade Trotsky's theory as such.

Comrade Trotsky presents the question in the following manner.

The theory of permanent revolution is a theory the principles of which were laid down by Karl Marx. 'Permanent Revolution', that is, 'unceasing revolution' is a revolution which in the last analysis has its limits in the achievement of

Socialist society. On the strength of this, Comrade Trotsky, in a number of his recent works, says: Very well, that is precisely what has happened — permanent revolution has justified itself *because the proletariat in Russia has captured political power.* Up till 1917 the Bolsheviks argued against the theory of permanent revolution; they constantly insisted that the revolution in Russia will be a bourgeois revolution. Indeed, in 1905 and up till the February revolution, we did say so. But who proved to be correct? The advocates of the theory of permanent revolution or the orthodox Bolsheviks? *The advocates of the theory of permanent revolution proved to be correct,* and the Bolsheviks *became 'good'* only in 1917 *because* they abandoned the Bolshevik theory of the revolution, and accepted the Trotskian interpretation.

These are the conclusions that Comrade Trotsky draws. Let us examine them.

First of all, it should be observed that the quintessence of the theory of permanent revolution is by no means the fact that we are confronted by revolution *which in the last analysis will reach a stage when the workers will have captured political power.* In *this* sense permanent revolution did come about, for the working class really came into power. [4] But here we have *another* question. And it is just this *other* question that represents the *'quintessence'* of the theory of permanent revolution. And it is of this quintessence that we must speak in the first place. But before doing so, it is necessary to state how Marx understood the theory of permanent revolution. In his pamphlet, Comrade Stalin quotes a decisive passage from Marx, and makes quite a correct commentary upon it. Marx wrote:

While the democratic petty bourgeois desires simultaneously to secure as great a number as possible of the above-mentioned demands, and to bring revolution to an end as speedily as possible, our interests and our tasks demand that the revolution shall become *unceasing until all the more or less wealthy classes have been removed from power and until the*

13

proletariat has captured political power. (Karl Marx and Friedrich Engels, Volume 3, Gosizdat, 1921, p 501) [5]

What then did Marx understand by the theory of uninterrupted revolution? By uninterrupted revolution Marx conceived the prospect of the revolution taking a course in which the relation of forces continuously changes, and the revolution all the time develops 'in an ascending line' [of a chart — translator]. The landlords, let us say, are overthrown. Their place is taken by one of the sections of the bourgeoisie, the liberal bourgeoisie, for example. With this the revolution does not end. The liberal bourgeoisie is overthrown and its place is taken by the radical petty bourgeoisie. The radical petty bourgeoisie is overthrown, and its place is taken by the poor class of the cities in the special meaning of the term, in alliance with the poor peasantry and the working class. Finally, even this government departs and gives place to the government of the working class. Of course, this is only a chart, as it were, of the process, but the chart is a correct one. [6] What then is the essence of the theory of permanent revolution?

The essence of the Marxian, that is, the *correct* theory of permanent revolution is that the constant changes in the social content of the revolution are taken into account. It reflects the fact that, in the progress of the revolution, the relation between the conflicting classes constantly changes, and that the revolution in its development constantly marches from one stage to another. It marches from the stage of feudalism to the liberal bourgeois stages. It advances from the liberal bourgeois stage to the petty bourgeois stage, and from that it advances to the stage of the proletarian revolution. This is the meaning of the Marxian (and not the Trotskian) theory of permanent revolution.

Can we have any objection to *such* a theory? No, for it is a correct one. In *this* sense, our revolution proved to be 'uninterrupted'. In Russia the revolution passed through a series of stages. In February, 1917, we had a substitution of the *landlord* regime by the liberal government of the imperialist bourgeoisie accompanied by the establishment of a parallel authority of the workers and peasants (the Soviets). Then followed a fresh regrouping, when the place of the liberal bourgeoisie was taken by various factions of the petty bourgeoisie in alliance with the liberals ('the Coalition Government' with the Mensheviks, Socialist Revolutionaries, etc). After that, when we took power in October the Bolsheviks and Left Socialist Revolutionaries came into power. After the revolt of the Socialist Revolutionaries, another change took place, and our Party became the sole government party. Thus in Russia, the curve of the revolution, taken as a whole, ascended all the time. (We say 'taken as a whole', because in the period of this advancing progress of the revolution, there were some minor halts. It is sufficient to recall the July days. This circumstance must be borne in mind because it is of no small importance in practice.)

This process found its expression in the structure of the state, in the transition of power from one class to another, from one social group to another, until a permanent position was reached by the *working class* taking power when the *dictatorship of the workers* established a firm foundation for itself and when the Communist Party became the only party holding political power in its hands. If we approach the question in *this manner*, that is, from the point of view of the actual progress of historical events, and we ask ourselves — does this represent the quintessence of the *Trotskian* permanent revolution? — we should have to reply — No. *And it is precisely this 'No' that is the 'nigger in the wood pile'* [sic — MIA] [7]. We will approach this *central* question from various points of view. For the moment we will merely draw the fundamental outline of what will serve as the subject of our further exposition.

Had Comrade Trotsky pictured to himself the situation in accordance with the *facts* as they afterwards appeared, he would not in 1905 have put forward the slogans which he did in conjunction with Parvus. As we know, in 1905, Comrade Trotsky put forward against the Bolsheviks the slogan: 'Down with the Czar, Up with the Government of the Workers!' In other words, Comrade Trotsky in 1905, at the *first* stage of our revolutionary movement, put forward as an *immediate* slogan, a slogan which was fulfilled only at the *last* stage of this process. Comrade Trotsky had no connection with the actual state of affairs as they existed *at that time*. In other words, the fundamental political charge we make against *Trotsky's* theory of permanent revolution is that it ignores all the *intermediate stages, that is, precisely that which* distinguishes permanent revolution.

These various stages of the revolution in which various classes fulfill their task and pass away to give place to others, demand of us *special* slogans applicable to each of these stages, directed towards a single goal. *Only in this way* can revolution be conducted. Comrade Trotsky, however, placed the final link of the revolution in the beginning of the chain when there were no grounds at all for doing so. He *leaped across* a number of intervening stages, and had our Party followed the lead of Comrade Trotsky, and had not conducted the revolution in the manner in which it did, we would simply have collapsed. Curious as it may seem, as a matter of fact, Comrade Trotsky *killed* the idea of permanent revolution, for if the 'end' is placed at the beginning, no process can take place; there are no transitions, no 'uninterrupted revolution'.

Did Comrade Trotsky understand the *peculiarities* of our Revolution? Did Comrade Trotsky see how each stage *passed* on, 'grew into' to [sic — MIA] the other? Was he able to 'seize upon' the *necessary link*? All these questions must be replied to in the negative. Comrade Trotsky presented the question in a very simplified form: in Russia only a proletarian revolution is possible (Comrade Trotsky *denied* the possibility of a bourgeois revolution even in 1905):

In Russia *only* a proletarian revolution is possible, but

16

this proletarian revolution in a petty bourgeois country is doomed unless it receives *state aid* from the victorious proletariat of Western Europe. Without direct *state aid* [italics ours — NB] of the European proletariat, the working class of Russia will not be able to maintain power and convert its temporary domination into a prolonged Socialistic dictatorship. *Of this there can be no doubt for a single moment.* (*Our Revolution*) [8]

Comrade Trotsky *began* by failing to understand the *peculiar process* of our revolution, a peculiarity which consisted in the curious interweaving of a *peasant war* against the landlords with a *proletarian revolution.* Comrade Trotsky failed to understand *the peculiarity of the first stage* of this revolution which consisted in the path being clear of feudalism and in the *break-up of big private land ownership* ('the agrarian question represents the foundation of the bourgeois revolution in Russia, and determines the national peculiarity of this revolution... The experience of the first period of the Russian Revolution has finally proved that it can be inevitable only as a peasant agrarian revolution.') [9]

Comrade Trotsky 'failed to observe' *the stages* by which the bourgeois revolution in Russia *grew into* a Socialist-proletarian revolution. Furthermore, Comrade Trotsky failed to see the *peculiarities* which distinguish our Socialist revolution from the Socialist revolutions in other countries.

Again, Comrade Trotsky failed to see the special *international* conditions which — even *without* the state aid of the victorious Western European proletariat — permit our Socialist revolution to *hold on,* to consolidate its position, and to *grow,* ultimately to triumph, together with the victorious working class of other countries. Even here, Comrade Trotsky reasons according to a chart: *either* a bourgeois revolution *or* a proletarian revolution; *either* a classical proletarian revolution — in that case permanent victory, *or* a hybrid proletarian revolution, in that case, death. *Either* state aid by the Western

17

European proletariat — in that case salvation, *or* no such aid — in that case there is no salvation.

As a matter of fact experience completely refuted this chart and gave altogether *different* replies. *Both* bourgeois *and* proletarian revolution (one merges into the other), *no* state aid from the Western proletariat, *but for all that* aid was forthcoming both from the proletariat and from the colonies (and also 'aid' from the capitalists, who by their internecine *quarrels* assist proletarian states). *No* classical proletarian revolution and yet not death, but life, etc. Reality proved *more full of colour* than the dry charts and carefully drawn diagrams of 'permanent revolution'.

Comrade Trotsky's *political impotence* originated in his failure to see actual facts. Because Lenin and our Party saw all these stages, transitions and peculiarities of the process they were *really able* on each occasion to seize the *necessary* link and lead the working class and the peasantry to victory. There are absolutely no grounds for our Party substituting the Leninist theory of our revolution by the 'permanent' theory of Comrade Trotsky.

General Estimate of Classes in the Progress of Our Revolution

We spoke above of the stages of our revolution. Now it is necessary to raise the same question, and in the same general form, but to examine it from the standpoint of *the struggle of classes* and *class changes*. The controversy among us, as is known to a considerable degree, centered around [sic — MIA] the question of the *Workers' and Peasants' Alliance*, the question of an alliance between the working class and the peasantry, and the question of the hegemony of the proletariat in this 'alliance'. Now, in the eighth year of our revolution and our dictatorship, we clearly see the *enormity* [sic — MIA] of this problem, which for the first time was distinctly outlined by Comrade Lenin and which later became one of the corner-stones both of the theoretical and practical structure of Bolshevism.

Only at the present time has this question come up in all its enormous dimensions. For, essentially the discussion concerns not only the problem of unity between the peasants and workers here, in Russia, in the Soviet Republics, but it concerns the greatest and, in a sense, the decisive problem of *the international revolution*. Such a burning question of modern times as the question of *the colonies*, which is a question of the life and death of capitalism, is, from the point of view of world revolution, nothing more nor less than the question of the unity between the Western European and American industrial proletariat on the one hand, and the colonial peasantry on the other.

It is true that the colonial question, although to a considerable degree a question of attitude towards the peasantry, is not wholly confined to this. It has its definite peculiar features, and it would be wrong to place it under the mark of complete equality. At the same time, it is absolutely clear that, in its social basis, it is a peasant question. If we ask ourselves in what manner the working class at the present moment can undermine the bases of capitalist society, we may say that the working class, which supports colonial rebellion, is actually imposing its hegemony on the peasant colonial movement. When we ask ourselves what will happen in the sphere of world economy when the working class captures power, immediately the same question arises as to the attitude of the victorious proletariat towards the colonial peasantry. When we ask ourselves why European Social-Democracy absolutely fails to understand the significance of the peasant question, and paid so little attention to it, and failed to raise the problem which was so characteristic for us, we do not merely raise the point that our country was an agrarian country, and the other countries were industrial. The other countries too, had their 'agrarian supplement', only they were not in the home countries, but in the remote colonies.

The fact that European Social-Democracy paid inadequate attention to the peasant question is undoubtedly connected with the circumstances that it failed to present the question of the *colonies* from the revolutionary standpoint. The policy of the Social-Democrats was either directly hostile to the colonial movements (social imperialism) or adopted a reticent policy. When Comrade Trotsky absorbed in his 'Europeanism' repeatedly emphasizes the Asiatic peasant character of the ideology of the 'immature' proletariat (this was precisely his estimation of the Bolsheviks) there was something in his 'Europeanism' that smacked of the contempt which the Social-Democrats bore towards the peasant and colonial question, although Comrade Trotsky personally devoted considerable attention to this question.

If Comrade Trotsky substitutes abstract schemes for concrete analysis, it must result in conceiving the proletarian revolution as a classical revolution, and regarding all 'non-classical' revolutions as being doomed beforehand. But a classical proletarian revolution in which the proletariat is the only class of the 'people' in other words, such an ideal revolution is possible only in a society where there is no peasantry.

Such an 'ideal' conception is totally out of harmony with reality. If we examine world economy we will find that the proletariat in the strict sense of the term represents a small minority of the population. If we have in mind the largest countries in the world, we must remember that these represent small sections of densely populated and proletarianised centres in enormous peasant colonies. The greatest part of France is in *Africa*, the greatest part of Britain is in *Asia*, etc. What will the British proletariat do after their victory if they do not receive the support and sympathy of the Indian and Egyptian peasants — if it does not lead them into the fight against capitalism, if it does not establish its *hegemony, its leadership*, over this enormous mass of humanity?

It is most amazing. Comrade Trotsky knows very well the enormous significance of the colonial question. But alas, this correct view of the colonies cannot possibly be reconciled with the estimation of the peasantry which Comrade Trotsky made in 1905, in his theory of permanent revolution, the correctness of which he stubbornly insists upon up to the present day. Comrade Trotsky reveals a complete lack of logic.

It is perfectly clear now what this problem means for the proletariat. Prior to the seizure of power the working class must obtain the support of the peasantry in the fight *against the capitalists and landlords*. After the seizure of power, the proletariat must secure for itself the support of a considerable section of the peasantry in *the civil war*, right up to the moment when the proletarian dictatorship has been consolidated. And after that? Can we really limit ourselves to regarding the peasantry merely as cannon-fodder in the fight against the capitalists and the large landlords? *No!* And once and for all, we must understand the logic of this *No*. After the victory, the

22

proletariat at all costs must live side by side with the peasantry, for the peasantry represents the majority of the population and has great economic and social weight. Only the failure to understand world economic ties can lead one to ignore this aspect of the question. But sooner or later it will inevitably come up. Consequently, it must be realized that the proletariat has no choice. It is compelled to carry the peasantry with it in its work of constructing Socialism. The proletariat *must learn* to do this, for unless it does so, it will not be able to maintain its rule.

Of course, there are various ways of leading the peasantry in accordance with the given circumstances. One must be able to see the transition points and all the stages in order to lead correctly. During the discussion on the question of the trade unions, Lenin wrote:

The whole of the dictatorship of the proletariat is a transition period, but the present time is, as it were, a heap of new transition periods. The demobilization of the army, the end of the war and the possibility of a more prolonged peaceful respite than we have had hitherto, a more permanent transition from the military front. *From these facts alone the relation of the proletariat to the peasantry has changed.* [10]

The same thing, but to an even greater degree, applies to a number of most important stages of the revolutionary process.

Comrade Trotsky, in his theory of permanent revolution, completely failed to understand:

1. The very problem of the peasantry.
2. The methods by which the proletariat could lead the peasantry.
3. The various stages in the relations between the working class and the peasantry in the course of our revolution.

Comrade Trotsky himself presents the question of the peasantry in great relief in the preface to his book *1905.*

Formulating the theory of permanent revolution (in 1922) and emphasizing the correctness of this theory, Comrade Trotsky wrote:

In order to secure its victory, the proletarian vanguard, in the first period of its rule, will have to make deep inroads not only into feudal, but into bourgeois property. In this *it will come into conflict not only with all the sections of the bourgeoisie... but also with the broad masses of the peasantry, with whose cooperation it came into power.* This contradiction in the position of a workers' government in a backward country, with an overwhelmingly peasant population, can be solved only on an international scale, in the arena of the world proletarian revolution. Compelled by historic necessity to break down the limitations of the bourgeois-democratic framework of the Russian revolution, the victorious proletariat will be compelled also to break down its national state limitations, that is, it will consciously strive to convert the Russian revolution into a prologue of the world revolution. [11]

The latter part of this quotation is correct. But that is not the point. The point is that according to Comrade Trotsky, the proletariat *must inevitably* come into irreconcilable conflicts *with the broad masses of the peasantry,* that in a country with a petty bourgeois majority, the proletariat will not be able to handle this problem and that as a result of this inevitable *conflict* the proletarian domination must collapse unless it can obtain *state* aid from outside.

The first thing one observes (at the moment after considerable experience has been accumulated of the *international* movement), is that Comrade Trotsky's 'solution' is not a solution at all, just as his 'permanent revolution' in fact is not permanent revolution at all. For, if the conflict between the proletariat and the peasantry is inevitable and unavoidable, etc, therefore, it is inevitable and unavoidable even in the case of the victory of the proletariat all over the world. The peasantry represents an enormous majority of the population of our planet.

If the proletariat has not the means by which to lead this peasantry, then, *either* the international revolution is also doomed, *or* it must be postponed (as Kunow [12] says) until we have a proletarian majority throughout the world. We can hardly believe that we will have to break down the 'terrestrial frontiers' and expect aid from the purely proletarian celestial forces, and 'state aid' at that.

Thus, if we develop the problem and present it in its full scope, it will be easily seen that Comrade Trotsky merely evades the problem, but does not solve it.

Comrade Trotsky's error lies in the fact that he considers the conflict between the proletariat and the peasantry as *inevitable*, whereas it is merely *possible*, and this is by no means the same thing. It will be inevitable if the proletarian regime proves to be less advantageous to the peasantry than was the bourgeois regime, and if the peasantry throws off the leadership of the proletariat. But it is not at all inevitable and *will not happen* if the Party of the victorious proletariat will make the corner-stone of its policy solicitude for the maintenance and strengthening of the workers and peasant alliance. The consideration of *how* this is to be done correctly is beyond the limits of this work.

From the estimation of the peasantry given above, follows the general *methods of influencing it*, which, by the by, Comrade Trotsky formulated in the period of reaction. This is what Comrade Lenin wrote on this matter:

Finally, *the least correct of all* is the third of the opinions of Comrade Trotsky quoted by Comrade Martov which appears to Comrade Martov to be reasonable: 'Even if it [the peasantry] will do this ['associate itself with the labour democratic regime'] with no more consciousness than it usually associates itself with the bourgeois regime *the proletariat can neither calculate on the ignorance and prejudices of the peasantry, as did the lords of the bourgeois regime, nor presume that the customary ignorance and passivity of the peasantry will be maintained in the period of the revolution.* ('the Aim of the Struggle of the Proletariat in Our Revolution', *Collected Works*, Volume 11, part 1, p 229) [13]

And in the epoch of proletarian dictatorship when it was necessary to pass from words to deeds, when the situation was *particularly* difficult, Lenin wrote:

The greater the extent and scope of historic events, the greater the number of people that take part in them and the more profound the change we desire to bring about, the more necessary is it to rouse interest in these events, to rouse a *conscientious attitude towards them* and to convince *millions and tens of millions of the people* of the necessity for them. (From a speech delivered at the Council of Peoples' Commissaries on 22 December 1920, *Collected Works*, Volume 12, p 413) [14]

Does this not express an altogether different attitude towards the peasantry? And does not this attitude follow logically from the general estimation of the peasantry as an essential ally in the struggle of the proletariat? But, in order to be able to 'convince' the peasantry, we must be able to 'hook them' by the proper link, and here more than ever is revealed the incapacity of Trotskyism to *approach* this question properly.

In 1905, Trotsky evaded the agrarian revolution and failed to understand that this was the *outstanding feature of the epoch.* The Mensheviks also failed to understand this, and Lenin quite rightly pointed out that they in 'fighting the Narodniki were simply blind to the historically real and progressive *content* of the principles of the Narodniki as the theory of the petty bourgeois struggle of democratic capitalism against liberal-landlord capitalism', and Lenin described this 'idea' as 'monstrous', 'idiotic' and 'treacherous' ('Prussian and American Paths of Development: A Letter to Skvortzov', *Proletarian Revolution*, May 1924, p 178). [15]

Comrade Trotsky even now asserts that his estimation of

the driving forces of the revolution was correct, and that in it there was no 'leaping across the peasantry', and that he had no intention of 'underestimating' the peasantry, Trotsky is very angry with his critics on this account. He writes:

A favorite argument that became fashionable in some circles [!] recently, is to point to — indirectly on most occasions — my 'underestimation' of the role of the peasantry. In vain, however, would you seek an analysis of this question... *There was no attempt to 'leap across' the peasantry in my writings at that time.* (*The New Course*, pp 50-51, italics ours — NB) [16]

This is how Comrade Lenin estimated the position of Comrade Trotsky in 1915 during the period of the war:

Comrade Trotsky's curious theory takes from the Bolsheviks the call for a resolute revolutionary proletarian fight for the conquest of political power, and from the Mensheviks the 'denial' of the role of the peasantry... As a matter of fact, Trotsky is assisting the liberal-labour politicians of Russia, who, by 'denial' of the role of the peasantry, mean to *refuse* to rouse the peasantry to revolution. ('two Lines of Development of the Revolution', *Collected Works*, Volume 13, pp 213-14) [17]

Comrade Lenin then gives a brief but brilliant description of the stages of the revolution and the content of these stages and our tasks. He wrote:

And this [that is, rousing the peasantry] is the most important question of the moment. The proletariat is fighting and will bravely continue to fight for the conquest of power, for a republic for the confiscation of the land. *That is to say, for winning over the peasantry, to utilize its revolutionary force*, to secure the participation of the 'non-proletarian masses of the people' in the emancipation of *bourgeois* Russia from *military-feudal* 'imperialism' (Czarism). The proletariat will *immediately* [NB, italics ours] take advantage of the emancipation of bourgeois Russia from Czarism, and of the agrarian power of the landlords, not for the purpose of aiding

27

the working peasants in their struggle against the rural workers, but for the purpose of completing the Socialist revolution in alliance with the proletariat of Europe. [18]

Thus, in spite of Comrade Trotsky, Comrade Lenin considered that Trotsky's theory did underestimate the role of the peasantry, and however much Comrade Trotsky would like to evade the admission of this fundamental and cardinal error, he cannot evade it. One cannot play at hide and seek. One must clearly, precisely and definitely say who is *right*. For, it is perfectly clear that before us are two *different* theories. According to one theory, the peasantry is an ally. According to the other, he is an inevitable foe. According to one theory, it is possible for us to conduct a successful fight for the hegemony over the peasantry; according to the other theory, this must fail. According to one theory, a sharp conflict with the peasantry is inevitable; according to the other, this conflict may be avoided if our policy is cleverly conducted.

Is it not clear that this 'permanent' question of a 'permanent' theory is the 'permanent' contradiction between Trotskyism and Leninism?

Notes

Notes are by the author except where added by the MIA.

1. LD Trotsky, *The New Course*, Chapter 6 — MIA.

2. LD Trotsky, *1905*, Preface to the First Edition. Bukharin has condensed Trotsky's text somewhat — MIA.

3. This letter does not seem to have been published in any English-language collection. Mikhail Olminsky (real surname Aleksandrov, 1863-1933), a Bolshevik and historian noted for his studies of Russian absolutism, was head of the Istpart, the Commission on the History of the October Revolution and History of the Communist Party, and approached Trotsky in the early 1920s with the idea of publishing his collected works; he subsequently took part in the campaign against 'Trotskyism' — MIA.

4. One must bear in mind here the *relative* character of the conception 'unceasing', for unceasing in the sense of a continuous and uninterrupted zone of revolution did not occur. After the defeat of 1905-07 there was an interval of a *complete decade* before the 'second revolution' broke out. In his article 'Two Lines of Revolutions' (*Collected Works*, Volume 8, Part 2, p 213) Comrade Lenin wrote:

To reveal the relations of classes in the forthcoming revolution is the principal task of a revolutionary party... Comrade Trotsky in *Nashe Slovo* wrongly solves the problem by repeating his "original" theory of 1905 and refusing to *think out why for a whole decade events ignored this beautiful theory.* [VI Lenin, 'On the Two Lines in the Revolution', *Collected Works*, Volume 21, — MIA.]

Thus, in the first place, there was a temporary *interruption* in the 'uninterrupted' revolution. Secondly, this interruption and subsequent events *repudiated* Comrade Trotsky's theory and his estimation of class forces, for history gave the peasantry a place which had been beforehand excluded from Comrade Trotsky's conception. But of that we will deal in the text.

5. The title of the Marx and Engels collection is omitted in the original. Karl Marx, 'Address of the Central Committee to the Communist League',; cited in JV Stalin, *The Foundations of Leninism* — MIA.

6. However, it should be borne in mind that this chart cannot be applied 'absolutely' to actual conditions. Here, too, one must calculate the concrete relation of social forces, for example, the peculiarity of the Russian bourgeois-democratic revolution consisted in that it could be conducted to a

finish only in the fight against the liberal bourgeoisie, which, already prior to the victory over Czarism, had become a *counter-revolutionary force*. The failure to understand this led the Mensheviks to commit actual treachery. In this connection Lenin wrote:

These people [NB — Martinov and Martov in the new *Iskra*], really argue as if they desire to limit, to cut short, their fight for liberty... Such people — said the *Vperod* [NB — the organ of the Bolsheviks], like Philistines, vulgarise the well-known Marxian postulate of the three principal forces of the revolution in the nineteenth (and twentieth) century, and its three fundamental stages. This postulate is to the effect that the first stage of the revolution limits the powers of absolutism, thus satisfying the bourgeoisie. The second stage is the establishment of the republic, satisfying the 'people', that is, the peasantry and the petty bourgeoisie generally. The third stage is the Socialist revolution which alone can satisfy the proletariat. '*Taken as a whole, this picture is correct*', wrote *Vperod*. We have before us indeed, an ascent to three different stages on a chart; differing in accordance with the classes which at best may accompany us on this ascent. But if we understand this Marxian chart of three stages to mean that *before every ascent* we must measure off for ourselves a modest distance, for example, not more than one stage, if, according to this stage, before every ascent, 'we will draw up for ourselves a plan of activity in the revolutionary epoch, we will be nothing more than Philistine virtuosi'. (VI Lenin, *Collected Works*, Volume 4, p 209) [VI Lenin, 'On the Provisional Revolutionary Government', *Collected Works*, Volume 8, — MIA.]

In other words, we cannot apply the chart directly in every case. 'Leaps' are *possible*. It would be sheer Philistinism to deny *all* possibility of skipping stages. However:

Let not some cavilling reader draw the conclusion from what we have said that we advocate 'tactics' directed towards "inevitable leaps across stages *irrespective of the relation of social forces*. (Ibid, p 210)

Thus, 'in the last analysis' it is the *relation of social forces* and the calculation of these forces that determines. Fearlessly to lead *the revolution forward*, but at the same time to be able to start out from the given relation of social forces and in this manner actually to maintain *the leadership* in the revolution — these are the tactics of Leninism.

7. Bukharin's original Russian text will have to be consulted to see if the matter was expressed in a less offensive manner — MIA.

8. LD Trotsky, *Results and Prospects*, Chapter 8 — MIA.

9. From an unpublished chapter of the work of Comrade Lenin on the agrarian question. See *Proletarian Revolution*, 1924, no 28, pp 166-69. [VI

Lenin, 'The Agrarian Programme of Social-Democracy in the First Russian Revolution, 1905-1907', *Collected Works*, Volume 13 — MIA.]

10. VI Lenin, 'The Trade Unions, the Present Situation and Trotsky's Mistakes', *Collected Works*, Volume 32 — MIA.

11. LD Trotsky, *1905*, Preface to the First Edition — MIA.

12. A reference to Heinrich Cunow (1862-1936), a theoretician of the German Social Democratic Party, editor of *Die Neue Zeit* during 1917-23, and author of the revisionist work *Die Marxsche Geschichts, Gesellschafts und Staatstheorie* (two volumes, Berlin, 1920-21). See Bukharin's remarks about him at Historical Materialism - a System of Sociology . — MIA.

13. VI Lenin, 'The Aim of the Proletarian Struggle in Our Revolution', *Collected Works*, Volume 13 — MIA.

14. VI Lenin, 'Report on the Work of the Council of People's Commissars', *Collected Works*, Volume 31 — MIA.

15. VI Lenin, 'Letter to II Skvortsov-Stepanov', *Collected Works*, Volume 16 — MIA.

16. LD Trotsky, *The New Course*, Chapter 6 — MIA.

17. VI Lenin, 'On the Two Lines in the Revolution', *Collected Works*, Volume 21, — MIA.

v18. VI Lenin, 'On the Two Lines in the Revolution', *Collected Works*, Volume 21, — MIA.